JUST WALK

A Journey of Faith, Gratitude and Never Losing Hope

JUST WALK

A Journey of Faith, Gratitude and Never Losing Hope

AMARPREET SINGH PURI

Available on amazonkindle

Worldwide Published by

Pendown Press

PREMIUM BUSINESS PUBLISHER

PENDOWN PRESS LLP

An ISO 9001 & ISO 14001 Certified Co.,

Regd. Office: 3767A, Kanhaiya Nagar,
Tri Nagar, Delhi-110035

Ph.: 8130886000, 9650072927, 8595249536

E-mail: info@pendownpress.com

Branch Office: 1A/2A, 20, Hari Sadan, Ansari Road,
Daryaganj, New Delhi-110002

Ph.: 011-45794768

Website: PendownPress.com

Edition: 2026

Price: ₹ 399

ISBN: 978-93-7217-654-4

Layout and Cover Designed by Pendown Graphics Team

Table of Contents

Acknowledgments

This book exists because I did not walk alone.

I begin with gratitude for my parents. My father taught me discipline, responsibility, and calm endurance without ever needing to display it. My mother taught me faith not through words, but through the way she lived, prayed, suffered, and continued with dignity even during illness. Watching her shaped my understanding of strength more than anything else.

I owe a special and heartfelt thank you to **my wife**. She has been my quiet anchor through every phase of this journey. She stood beside me during uncertainty, long workdays, health scares, emotional exhaustion, and spiritual shifts, often without questions, without complaints, and without needing recognition. When I doubted myself, she held the ground steady. When life felt heavy, she carried more than her share so I could keep moving forward. This book carries her strength as much as it carries mine.

I am equally grateful to **my son,** who grew alongside this journey and gave me purpose beyond my own struggles. Their presence reminded me why it was important to keep walking, even on difficult days.

I acknowledge **the doctors who looked deeper when surface answers were not enough,** and whose honesty changed the course of my health journey. I thank the mentors and colleagues who trusted me before results could speak for themselves.

There are also people whose names may never appear here but whose presence mattered deeply: the house-help who cared for my bedridden mother with devotion and later faced her own battle with cancer, the clients who placed trust in me during uncertain beginnings, and the many individuals whose silent struggles reminded me that everyone is carrying something unseen.

This book is a reflection of all those lives that touched mine along the way.

Preface

I have walked through many phases of life without stopping to name them.

→ Some phases came with clarity.

→ Some came with fear.

→ Some came with silence.

→ And some came with questions I did not know how to answer at the time.

For a long while, I believed that life rewards those who plan well, move fast, and stay in control. Experience taught me otherwise.

Life often moves in ways we do not design.

It tests us through illness, responsibility, loss, and uncertainty. And in those moments, the only real choice we have is whether we keep moving or freeze in place.

→ This book is not about reaching somewhere extraordinary.

→ It is about continuing to walk when you do not know where the road leads.

If you are holding this book, I hope you read it slowly. Not to find answers, but to find permission, permission to move forward without certainty, to trust timing, and to believe that progress does not always look dramatic.

Sometimes, it simply looks like one step at a time.

I never planned to write a book.

I am not a writer by training, and I never saw myself as someone whose life needed to be documented.

For most of my years, I was focused on doing my work, fulfilling my responsibilities, and keeping my personal struggles private.

But over time, people began asking questions.

- How did I stay grounded during illness?
- How did I keep going when things were uncertain?
- How did faith enter my life without being forced?
- How did I manage responsibility without losing myself?

I realised that these questions were not about achievement. They were about survival, balance, and inner movement.

Just Walk was written from that space.

This book does not offer formulas or shortcuts.

It shares experiences, moments where life slowed me down, forced me inward, and taught me lessons that could not be learned any other way. The insights in these pages were shaped by hospitals, long walks, quiet prayers, professional setbacks, and unexpected grace.

If there is one message in this book, it is simple:

→ You do not need to have everything figured out to move forward.

→ Sometimes, walking itself becomes the answer.

Who Am I?

My name is Amarpreet Puri.

My professional journey has spanned multiple industries, from customer service and corporate training to export-driven manufacturing and moisture control solutions. I have spent decades working closely with people, listening to problems before offering solutions, and building trust through consistency rather than promises.

Outside of work, my life has been shaped deeply by experiences with illness, responsibility, faith, and recovery. Walking became more than a physical habit for me; it became a way to think, process, and remain grounded.

Just Walk is not written as an expert or a teacher. It is written as someone who has learned by living, stumbling, pausing, and continuing.

Why This Book?

This book was written for those who feel stuck waiting for clarity. I have learned that clarity often comes after movement, not before it. Many of us pause our lives waiting for certainty about health, career, purpose, or direction. We tell ourselves we will move once things make sense. But in my experience, life does not reward waiting. It responds to honest effort and quiet persistence.

There were phases in my own life where I waited for answers, from doctors, from work, from circumstances, from God. And most of the time, those answers did not arrive the way I expected.

What arrived instead were situations that demanded I keep going even without reassurance.

I learned, sometimes painfully, that stopping only deepens confusion. Movement, even slow and unsure movement, creates its own understanding over time.

Just Walk is not meant to inspire action for the sake of action. It is not about:

- Pushing harder
- Running faster
- Or chasing outcomes.

It is about choosing to move with awareness.

About taking the next step with sincerity, even when the destination is unclear. About trusting that effort, done with the right intention, eventually finds its place.

This book does not promise transformation. It speaks about endurance.

- → It speaks about responsibility, illness, faith, work, and the long stretches in between where nothing dramatic happens, but everything important is being shaped quietly.
- → It is written for people who are doing their best without applause, who are carrying responsibilities they did not choose, and who are learning to live with unanswered questions.

If you are reading this while going through a difficult phase, I want you to know that uncertainty does not mean you are lost. It often means you are in transition. And transitions require patience more than confidence.

- ➢ You do not need to fix your entire life at once.
- ➢ You do not need to understand everything today.
- ➢ You only need to keep moving honestly.

If this book helps you slow down without giving up, reflect without withdrawing, and walk forward without pretending to have all the answers, then it has done what it was meant to do.

- ➢ You are not behind.
- ➢ You are not late.
- ➢ You are not failing.

You are walking.

And sometimes, that is enough.

How to Read This Book?

There is no correct way to read this book.

You may read it from beginning to end, or return to certain chapters when life places you in similar phases.

- Some chapters may feel heavy
- Some may feel comforting
- Some may not resonate right now

Take your time.

→ Read slowly. Pause often. Reflect when needed.

→ Walk while reading, if that helps you think.

This book is not about reaching the end.

It is about staying in motion.

When you are unsure of the next step, remember, you do not need to see the entire path.

Just walk.

Chapter 1

Carrying More Than Childhood

I was never really a child.

Not in the way others were.

Most children begin their lives by being held. I began mine by being counted on.

My parents had prayed for years to have a son. Two daughters came first, both loved deeply, but the yearning for a boy lingered quietly in every corner of the house, in my father's silence, in my mother's folded hands before the Guru Granth Sahib, in every blessing whispered by visiting relatives.

When I finally arrived, they said it was God's mercy. I was their Mannat, a prayer answered, a promise fulfilled. The day I was born, people filled our home like it was a festival. My father distributed sweets at the Gurudwara.

From that moment, my place in the world was already decided.

I wasn't just a child; I was the continuation of a family name, the dream my parents had waited for.

But sometimes, when you're born as the answer to someone else's prayers, you forget to learn how to pray for yourself.

Even before I could walk, everyone reminded me of who I was supposed to become.

- "He will take care of the house."
- "He will make his parents proud."
- "He will do what his father couldn't."

Those words sounded like blessings. I only realised much later that they were also expectations, waiting patiently for me to grow into them.

My early years were surrounded by women.

Two elder sisters, two cousin sisters, our house was always full of laughter, chatter, and stories. They treated me like their little prince but also their little protector.

They shaped my earliest lessons in empathy. They also became the reason I learned early what pain looked like.

My childhood home was a modest one, a small world of faith, work, and quiet endurance. My father was a man of structure, not sentiment. He believed in doing, not expressing. His shoes were always polished, his words measured, his gaze steady. He rarely raised his voice, but when he spoke, we all listened. My mother was the opposite, soft where he was firm, spiritual where he was practical. She prayed before dawn, worked until her hands were sore, and smiled through every exhaustion. She never once let us see her cry.

Together, they taught me discipline and devotion, two things that would later save my life more than once.

But between them, I also learned something no one said aloud: that love can be heavy. It can come tied to duty, wrapped in silence, built on sacrifice.

By the time I was seven or eight, I could already sense that my family's hopes were stitched into my small shoulders. I didn't resent it. I didn't even understand it fully. But I could feel it, the quiet weight of needing to be someone important someday.

I remember my mother once saying, almost to herself, "He was born for a reason. God doesn't send children like this without purpose."

I didn't know what that reason was. But I began living as if I had to prove her right.

Then came the first real crack in childhood, the day my eldest sister got married.

It was a celebration that our family had waited for years. The house smelled of halwa and fresh marigolds. Music played from morning to night. My sisters danced, my father smiled, and my mother's eyes shone with tears and pride. I remember holding my sister's chooda bangles in my hands and thinking how beautiful she looked. Everyone said she was lucky. Everyone said she had found a good man.

But a few months later, something changed. Her laughter became rarer. Her phone calls shorter. The sparkle in her eyes dimmed into something quieter, something strained.

And then, one day, I saw in the moment that divided my life into "before" and "after."

She had come home after an argument. Her husband had followed soon after. I was there, standing at the edge of the room, when I saw the way he spoke to her, harsh, dismissive, stripping her dignity with words that made my blood run cold. My parents were there too, caught between tradition and truth, trying to hold the situation together without letting the world see the cracks.

I was too young to step in. But too aware to look away.

That night, I lay awake, staring at the ceiling, trying to make sense of what I had witnessed. The house was silent except for the faint sound of my mother crying in the next room. I didn't understand why the world allowed a woman so full of love to be treated that way.

Something hardened inside me that day. I realised that life was not fair, and that women often paid the highest price for other people's egos.

That was the day childhood ended for me.

After that, I stopped seeing myself as the youngest. I began to think of myself as a protector, even though I had no idea how to protect anyone yet. That moment planted a seed that would later grow into a quiet resolve: that no woman around me should ever feel unsafe, unseen, or unloved.

When you're a child, and your first encounter with pain comes from inside your own home, you learn early that strength is not a choice, it's a necessity.

In the years that followed, I became quieter. More observant. I watched how my mother continued to hold the family together despite everything. I noticed how my father's silence deepened, how he carried disappointment without complaint.

Our home looked normal from the outside, but I had begun to see the invisible work of love in the late nights, the compromises, the unspoken griefs that adults carry because life gives them no other option.

Being born as a mannat child meant I couldn't show weakness. Everyone believed I was destined for great things, the boy who would one day lift the family name higher. I carried that belief like a badge and a burden.

And yet, beneath it all, I was still a boy, confused, curious, wanting to play, wanting to understand the world that seemed to demand so much so soon.

I sometimes wonder if the pressure to "become" came from outside or from within me. Maybe both. Maybe once people tell you you're special, you start chasing the image even if it breaks you in the process.

Still, I wouldn't trade those years. They built the foundation of who I became: empathetic, responsible, and deeply aware of others' pain.

But they also came at a cost. I learned endurance before joy.

And when I finally stepped out of that protected world into school and adolescence, I carried with me not just my books, but the weight of everything I'd seen and felt.

That's when the next kind of struggle began, one that had nothing to do with family and everything to do with me.

- My health.
- My studies.
- My mind that refused to sit still.

The storms outside had ended for a while.

But inside me, a new one was just beginning.

The fracture did not weaken the story. It decided its direction.

Amarpreet Singh Puri

Chapter 2

The Storm Begins

When childhood ends early, school stops feeling like a playground. It becomes a place where you learn how to survive expectations.

By the time I reached school, I was already used to carrying more than my age would allow.

I was the Mannat child, the one who was prayed for, hoped for, expected to make everything right.

That invisible label followed me into every classroom, every exam, every conversation that began with, "He's the only son, he must do well."

But life has a way of humbling even your best intentions.

The very subjects that gave others confidence, Mathematics and Accounts, made me feel small. No matter how long I stared at the pages, numbers seemed to blur, rearranging themselves before my eyes. I would memorise, forget, re-learn, and still get stuck on the same problems.

- I thought I wasn't trying hard enough.
- Teachers thought I was careless.
- My father, disappointed but restrained, thought I lacked discipline.

The truth was, my mind didn't move in straight lines.

It raced ahead, jumped tracks, drifted into daydreams, and then came back too late to catch up.

I could grasp what others missed, yet miss what others never struggled with.

I was bright, curious, talkative, even creative, and yet, completely scattered inside.

My notebooks were messy. My report cards were unpredictable. Some teachers called me gifted. Others lazy. Both were half right.

I tried to fix myself by trying harder. But no matter how early I woke up or how long I sat at my desk, my thoughts kept slipping like sand through my fingers.

The frustration turned inward. I began to believe something was wrong with me.

There's a kind of loneliness that doesn't come from being alone. It comes from not understanding your own mind. From pretending to be "fine" when you're constantly fighting to stay focused, to stay present, to stay enough.

Some nights, I would lie awake listening to my parents talk softly in the next room, about money, about my marks, about what they could do differently.

My mother always defended me. "He's a good boy," she'd say, "He just needs more time."

But I could hear the worry in her voice. That worry became my shadow.

Then, just as life often does, it handed me something unexpected, something that softened the sharp edges.

Amid the academic confusion and the first signs of my body beginning to rebel, the fatigue, the stomach aches, the unexplained dizziness, I found comfort in something else: companionship.

I met her when I was in Class 11. She came from an Army background, confident yet kind, always on the move because of her father's postings.

I was the school's head boy then, a title that made me seem to have everything together.

But beneath that badge, I was crumbling quietly, trying to keep pace with a mind that refused to slow down.

She didn't know any of that.

She just saw me.

Not the marks. Not the mistakes. Just me.

It's strange how the right person, even briefly, can make you feel seen without asking you to explain yourself.

Our friendship was gentle, honest, almost sacred.

We talked after school, exchanged notes, and sometimes just walked home in silence.

No promises, no drama, just presence.

That connection became my quiet strength.

On the days I failed an exam or woke up with that dull ache in my body,

or felt like the world was sprinting ahead while I stood still, I remembered her steadiness. It kept me walking.

Still, life at home wasn't easy.

→ My father believed in structure.

→ My mother believed in patience.

Both believed in me, but neither could understand me.

And maybe that was the hardest part.

When your mind doesn't follow the world's rhythm, love doesn't always translate into understanding.

So I learned to hide my struggles, the sleepless nights, the blank exam sheets, the panic before every test.

I smiled through the confusion, laughed when I could, and pretended everything was fine.

But inside, I was always on edge.

The sound of a teacher calling my name could twist my stomach.

Even the smallest mistake could send me spiralling.

And yet, somewhere in that storm, I found something precious: persistence.

When you fail often enough, you learn how to stand up even when no one's watching.

You learn how to start again when the world expects you to quit.

- Every morning, I still walked to school.
- Stood in the assembly.
- Played the TABLA.
- Laughed with friends.
- Came home, tried again.

That rhythm became the foundation of my resilience.

By the time I finished school, I didn't have the best grades.

But I had something far rarer, the will to keep going.

It's only now, years later, that I understand what those days were really teaching me.

They taught me that failure isn't the opposite of growth but a part of it.

That strength isn't always loud. Sometimes it's the quiet decision to try again tomorrow.

That persistence often outlasts talent.

And that small joys can hold you steady even when the ground beneath you shakes.

But back then, I didn't see it that way.

Back then, I was just tired.

- Tired of being misunderstood.
- Tired of pretending to be someone I wasn't.
- Tired of trying to explain what I couldn't name.
- Tired of always being "almost there."

And then, one night, it happened.

A sudden, sharp pain tore through my body, deep, unfamiliar, and impossible to ignore. It felt as if something inside me had finally cracked open after years of quiet strain.

That night became the pause between who I was and who I was about to become.

The storm I had been carrying in my mind had finally found its way into my body.

And it would change everything.

Small joys can hold you steady even when the ground beneath you shakes.

Amarpreet Singh Puri

Chapter 3

The Choice to Stay

There are certain chapters in life that unfold so quietly, you only realise their significance years later. You think you're simply living through confusion or responsibility or love, and only afterwards do you see how those days were shaping the rest of your life.

For me, that chapter began with a long wait.

When I look back now, I realise that our story never followed the script people expect.

There was no neat timeline, no steady sequence of courtship, marriage, and stability. What there was, instead, was distance and a constant balancing act between duty and desire.

We had been committed to each other for a while, but marriage was always just a little beyond reach.

There were family obligations, delays, and hesitations. My father's health was deteriorating; he suffered from recurring kidney stone issues, and every few months, our household would slip into another cycle of hospital visits and quiet anxiety.

I had already switched from regular college to correspondence. At that time, it didn't feel like a choice; it felt like something I owed to my family. "You can always study later," I told myself. "Right now, you're needed here."

What I didn't realise was that in the process of showing up for everyone, I was slowly disappearing from myself.

It's strange how responsibility can look noble from the outside but feel like suffocation from the inside.

Amidst all this, there was she, waiting at the other end of it all. Our conversations were full of patience and hope, but also of restlessness.

→ She wanted a partner who could be present, not someone drifting between family obligations and philosophical escapes.

→ I, on the other hand, was trying to find peace in anything that could make sense of the chaos around me.

That search led me to spirituality.

It started innocently, a conversation with an old school friend who had been diagnosed with kidney failure when we were in the tenth standard. When I met him years later, he was living with the same condition, but what struck me was his calm. He wasn't bitter, he wasn't afraid, he was joyful.

"How?" I remember asking him.

"How can you be at peace when everything around you is so uncertain?"

He smiled and said something that stayed with me:

"Because I've stopped fighting with life.

Pain belongs to the body, not to the soul."

Those words unsettled me. They made me question everything: why I was so restless, why I felt trapped even when I was doing all the right things. I began attending spiritual discourses, meeting people who seemed untouched by the world's noise. For the first time in years, I could breathe.

But peace, I learnt later, can also be another form of escape.

The deeper I went, the more detached I became. There came a point when I genuinely thought I might never marry, that perhaps my purpose lay elsewhere. I even said it aloud once that I wanted to dedicate my life to spiritual service.

When I think of it now, it sounds like the confused idealism of a young man trying to make sense of pain. But at that time, I believed it completely.

And then, there was her, quietly watching, quietly waiting.

She didn't argue. She didn't accuse. She simply told me, one evening, in her usual calm way,

"If you're not here, I don't want to spend my life waiting for a part of you that never arrives."

There was no anger in her voice, but something in that sentence shook me. For the first time, I realised how deeply my absence had begun to hurt her.

I was calling it spirituality; she saw it as distance.

It takes love to stay, but it takes courage to demand presence.

That conversation became the first mirror I ever looked into, honestly. It forced me to confront the difference between detachment and avoidance. I began to see how easily I had used "peace" as an excuse to not face my responsibilities. She wasn't rejecting my beliefs; she was reminding me that faith means nothing if it doesn't ground you in life.

And then, before we could even find a rhythm again, life intervened in the most brutal way possible.

Our engagement had just been fixed. There was relief in the air as if all the waiting had finally led somewhere. Ten days later, I met with a severe accident.

My right leg was fractured in twenty-eight places.

Everything stopped.

The pain was unbearable, but the helplessness was worse. I had always prided myself on movement, on taking charge, on doing things for others. Now, I couldn't even walk to the door without support. My mother would sit near my bed, silently praying. My father, already unwell, looked older overnight. And somewhere in all that heaviness, I felt like I had failed everyone again, especially her.

It would have been so easy for her to step away then.

She had every reason to. Her family had every reason to. There were doubts about my health, my future, and my stability. What if I didn't recover properly? What if I couldn't provide? What if life with me was going to be nothing but hospitals and responsibility?

But she didn't leave. She stayed.

Not in the dramatic, cinematic sense but in the quiet, everyday ways that matter more than grand gestures. She would call, visit, check on me, and never once make me feel like a burden. She didn't treat my injury as a weakness. She treated it as a phase, one we would get through together.

There's a certain grace in that kind of loyalty. It doesn't announce itself. It just stands there, steady, when everything else falls apart.

Looking back now, I think that accident was more than a physical injury. It was a turning point. Until then, I had been trying to find peace outside of responsibility. After that, I began to see that maybe peace comes from showing up where life has placed you, not running from it.

Her faith in me made me return to myself.

She had asked for nothing, not comfort, not wealth, not even promises.

She had only asked for one thing: presence.

And that became the foundation of our marriage.

Even now, years later, I don't think love is something you prove in easy times. It's proven in the moments when you have every reason to walk away, and you still choose to stay. She did that. Quietly, without expectation, without applause.

When people ask me what defines our relationship, I don't think of dates or anniversaries. I think of that one line she said to me, the one that changed everything:

"If you're not here, I don't want to spend my life waiting for a part of you that never arrives."

It took me years to understand the full meaning of that sentence.

It wasn't a complaint.

It was a reminder that love isn't about possession, it's about presence. And sometimes, the person who saves your life doesn't do it by lifting you, but by refusing to let you disappear.

That's what she did for me.

And that's when I finally became capable of loving her back, not as a man looking for escape, but as someone who had finally learnt how to stay.

I don't think love is something
you prove in easy times.

It's proven in the moments
when you have every reason t
walk away, and you still
choose to stay.

Amarpreet Singh Puri

Chapter 4

Finding My Own Work

When I think about how my career began, it never feels like a single clean moment when everything started. It feels more like a slow drift. A series of small decisions that, at the time, did not look important at all.

After college, it was almost natural that I would step into work.

There was no phase in my life where I sat and "explored options" the way people do today. We did not have that language. We had responsibilities. There was a thriving business, regular customers, material going out to printing presses across India, and always something that needed to be handled.

I joined that flow because it was the obvious thing to do.

For a while, I travelled with the routine. Tours, visits, orders, follow-ups. On the surface, it looked like a stable path. I was learning how trade worked, how relationships were maintained, how credit cycles and supply chains were managed. But somewhere inside, a restlessness stayed. I could not see myself doing the same thing in the same way for the next twenty or thirty years.

The work was honest, but I did not feel connected to it. It felt like I was walking in someone else's shoes, trying to make them fit.

I still remember a long work trip, around twenty-five days, when this feeling became hard to ignore. Every day looked the same: trains, buses, small hotels, meetings in offices that smelled of paper and ink. We would talk about rates, quantities, and timelines. People were kind enough, respectful enough, but I could feel my energy shrinking. I began to realise that if I stayed in that pattern, I would slowly switch off from myself.

Nothing was exactly wrong, but nothing felt right either.

When I came back home after that trip, something in me had already decided that I needed to step out. I did not make a big announcement. I just knew, quietly, that I wanted to find work where I could grow on my own terms, learn something new, and not simply walk on an already-made track.

Around that time, call centres and BPOs were becoming a big thing in India. You would hear young people talk about “night shifts,” “international process,” and salaries that sounded exciting for someone just starting out. For me, it represented something else: exposure. A chance to understand a different world. A chance to prove myself without anyone’s support.

So I did what thousands of others were doing then: I printed my CV and started giving interviews.

This is where the story usually gets simplified in most people’s minds. They imagine you apply, you get selected, and you start working.

My reality was completely different. Before I got that first job, I must have given between 50 to 70 interviews.

It was a mix of written tests, group discussions, personal interviews, and hours spent waiting in lobbies with bright lights and glass doors, only to be told, “We’ll let you know,” and then never hearing back.

- Sometimes the reason was my accent.
- Sometimes it was my experience.
- Sometimes they simply didn’t say why.

At first, each rejection hurt. After a while, they became a familiar part of the process. I would feel disappointed for a few minutes, then pick up my folder and move on to the next one.

Looking back, that phase toughened me in a quiet way. It taught me how to walk into rooms where nobody knew me, answer questions from strangers, and still hold my ground even when the outcome wasn't in my favour.

It also made the first "yes" deeply meaningful.

When I finally got selected for a call centre job with a well-known group, it did not feel like a small step.

For me, it was a doorway into a completely different world.

The first thing that struck me was the training. Up until then, no one had ever spoken to me about how to sit, how to speak on the phone, how to respond under pressure, or how to listen properly. In this job, they trained us on everything. Voice and accent. Customer handling. Grooming. Corporate etiquette.

It felt as if someone had pressed a reset button on how I presented myself to the world.

We learned to speak clearly, to pace our words, and to sound calm even when the person on the other end of the line was frustrated or rude. We learned how to take responsibility without taking things personally. At that age, this kind of structured training was a gift. It changed the way I saw myself.

I was no longer just someone trying to get a job. I was a professional being shaped for global interactions.

Over time, I didn't just survive in that environment; I grew in it.

I was promoted. I got certificates of appreciation. I was trusted with more responsibility. I had the opportunity to train others in voice, accent and customer service. The boy who had once been unsure if he would get any job at all was now teaching people how to speak to customers across the world. That confidence stayed with me.

Those years in the BPO world were more than a paycheck.

- They polished me.
- They gave me structure.
- They made me comfortable with communication, technology, systems, and people from different backgrounds.
- They prepared me for roles I did not even know were coming.

My shift into the desiccant and packaging world did not happen through a grand plan. It happened because one opportunity led to another.

Through a buying agency, I was introduced to a company that supplied silica gel and desiccants to exporters. It sounded technical and small at first. Most people don't think about what protects goods inside a container or a carton. They think about the product, not the small pouches inside. But the more I listened, the more I understood how critical that "small" part actually was.

This buying house worked with around four hundred exporters. They supplied major handicraft and textile retailers abroad, with store chains spread across the US and Canada. Their exporters were constantly grappling with moisture, long-distance shipments, and inconsistent vendor quality. If the desiccant failed, the goods were at risk. And if the goods were damaged, the losses were huge.

I joined the company as the sales and marketing person. It was not a big team with separate departments. It was more like: here is the product, here is the market, here are the problems, now see what you can do. It suited me.

My call centre background helped more than any formal qualification could have.

I knew how to listen patiently, how to ask the right questions, how to understand what someone was really worried about, even if they did not say it directly. Exporters were not just looking for a supplier. They were looking for reliability, timely dispatch, consistent quality, and someone who would respond promptly when an issue arose.

In the very first month, a significant opportunity arose. The global buying house was evaluating suppliers for their desiccant requirement. They needed someone organised, responsive, and capable of handling volume and documentation. We started with samples and discussions. We answered technical questions. We adjusted where required. We showed we were willing to work to their standards, not just ours.

When that deal finally went through, it changed everything. Overnight, our small operation was connected to four hundred exporters through one central relationship.

- For the company, it was a major step.
- For me, it was confirmation that I could handle responsibility at that level.

From there, my role became deeper. I was the one writing emails, setting up basic systems, creating Excel sheets, tracking orders, responding to queries, and slowly building a network. I insisted on proper internet and a laptop in the office, even though it still wasn't standard everywhere. I knew we couldn't manage global expectations if we were stuck in slow, manual ways of working.

It wasn't glamorous work. A lot of it was quiet: replying to emails, coordinating with production, checking dispatches, understanding feedback, and staying late when needed. But I enjoyed it. For the first time, I could see a clear connection between my efforts and a business's growth. If I handled a relationship well, solved a problem on time, and followed up properly, it showed in trust, repeat orders, and reputation.

What started as "just a job" slowly began to feel like something I was meant to be part of.

I was no longer thinking of myself only as an employee. Without realising it, I had started thinking like someone who carried a stake in the outcome. Not on paper yet, but internally.

The journey from that point to being eventually offered a partnership is a story in itself. That phase brought its own turning points, its own tests, its own miracles. But this chapter belongs to the earlier years when I was still finding my feet, learning how the world of work operates, and discovering that with the right mindset, even a rejected candidate with no connections can build a meaningful career.

At that time, I did not know where all of this would lead. I only knew one thing: whenever life placed a door in front of me, I was willing to knock, even if I had heard "no" many times before. In the end, that willingness made all the difference.

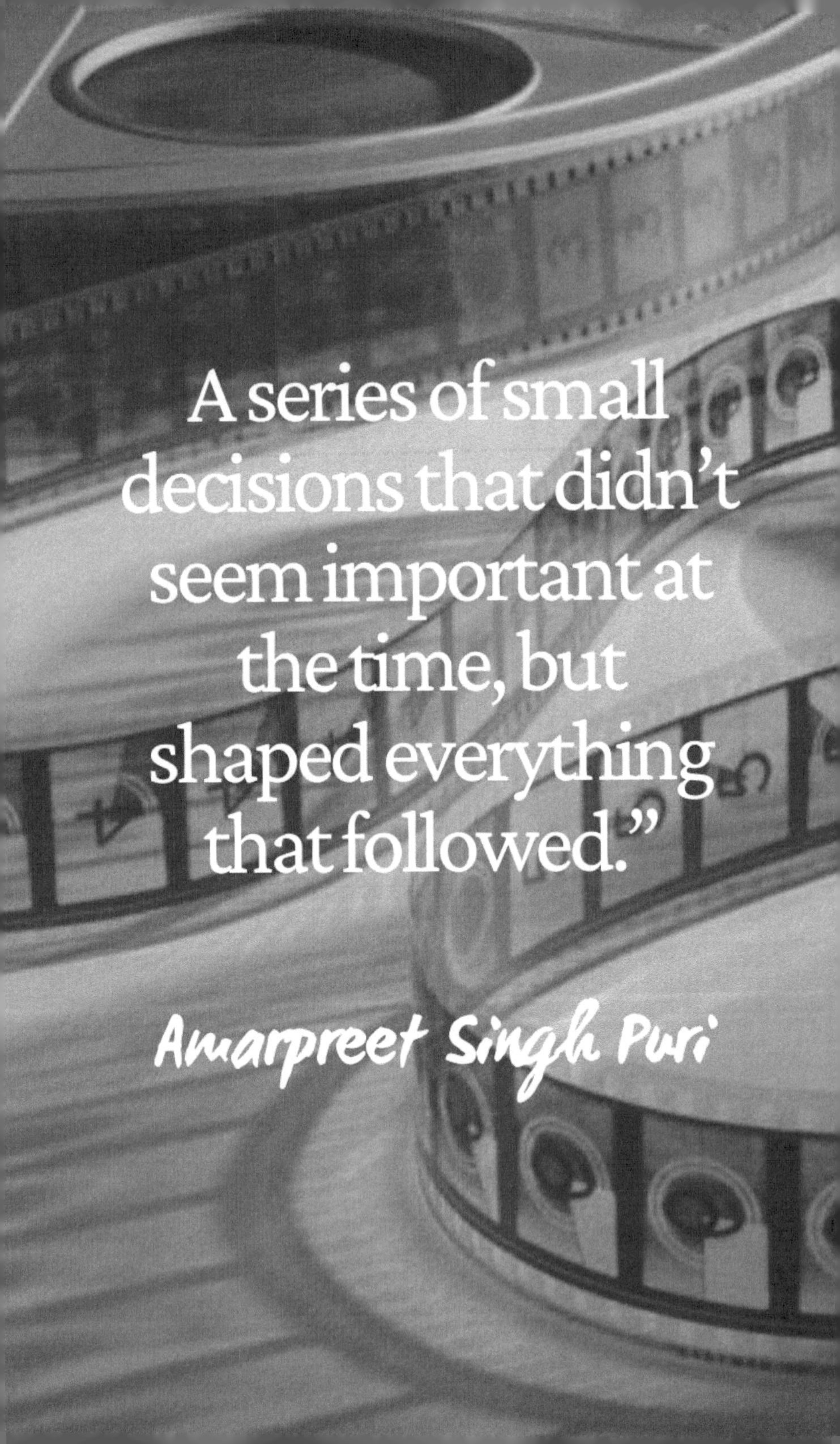
A series of small decisions that didn't seem important at the time, but shaped everything that followed."
Amarpreet Singh Puri

Chapter 5

The Path Inward

My spiritual journey didn't begin on a mountain, in a temple, or before a saint. It began in rooms where life felt heavier than my age could handle.

Looking back, I realise I never "chose" spirituality the way people choose hobbies or habits. It came to me slowly, through people, through pain, through quiet moments where there was nothing left to rely on except faith.

Growing up, I wasn't very religious.

My father was deeply so. He would wake up before dawn, sit in front of Guru Granth Sahib, and pray softly while the rest of the house slept. My father wasn't expressive about it, but he believed in discipline, in doing things the right way, in karma. I observed both of them, but I never truly absorbed them back then. Life was simple. My concerns were basic. I didn't need God; I needed answers to small questions.

All of that changed when my mother fell seriously ill.

When my father passed away, faith stopped being inherited and became personal.

Until then, spirituality had always lived outside me, something I had observed in him, in his discipline, in his quiet mornings before the Guru Granth Sahib. After his death, there was no one left to carry that belief on my behalf. Grief stripped away distance. In his absence, I understood that faith is not something you watch; it is something you step into when there is no one left to lean on. What he had practiced silently for years, I was now forced to understand in my own way.

Watching someone you love lie helplessly on a bed strips you of every illusion of control.

For the first time, I understood how fragile life is and how little we can actually do when the body stops listening. The house help who cared for her became a blessing we never expected, but even with her support, there were nights when the fear was too much to handle.

Those months forced something to open inside me. When you have no certainty, no timeline, no doctor giving you hope, you automatically turn inward.

I found myself praying, not with ritual, but with desperation. Not asking for miracles, but asking for strength.

Then came her recovery, slow but steady, almost against medical logic.

And soon after that came the shock of our house help's cancer diagnosis.

Two women. Both fighting for their lives in different ways. Both showing more courage than anyone expected. Watching them made something shift inside me.

Spirituality stopped being a concept. It became a necessity.

Years later, when I faced my own health challenges, everything I had learned from those women came back to me. Kidney problems don't arrive politely. They come with pain, exhaustion, and a fear that sits quietly at the back of your mind. I remember tests, scans, doctors shrugging, uncertainty piling up month after month.

There were periods where I felt fine and periods where I felt something inside me was shutting down. At one point, my reports were almost hopeless. The doctors suspected kidney failure. There were long days when I tried to appear normal, keep working, and hide the fear I didn't want my family to see.

And then there was that moment.

A day during a spiritual gathering, surrounded by Simran and kirtan, when something inside me loosened. I can't explain it medically, and I won't try. All I know is that in those twenty minutes, it felt like something was being cleared, emotionally first, physically later. When I came out of that room, I felt lighter. Peaceful in a way I hadn't felt in months.

More importantly, my next medical report came back clean.

I didn't scream "miracle." I didn't run around telling people what happened. But inside me, something changed permanently.

Faith, which had entered my life quietly years ago, now had a place to stay.

Spirituality, for me, has never been about rituals. I don't sit with a fixed timetable. I don't make promises to God when I want something. I don't bargain, and I don't threaten. My spiritualism is simple:

Show up with honesty. Do the work with sincerity. Accept what comes. Let go of what you cannot control.

I believe God works through timing. Through people. Through instinct.Through small nudges that push you toward the right door.

There were many times in life when I thought I was making

decisions logically, but looking back, I realise something else was guiding me. When I left the family trade, when I tried the call centre route despite dozens of rejections, when I entered the desiccant industry without knowing a thing about it, when I survived my health struggles, none of it felt planned. But all of it felt directed.

I've stopped calling it luck.

It isn't luck when it keeps happening. It isn't a coincidence that every closed door leads to something better. It isn't a chance when the right people appear exactly when they should.

I call it grace. Simple, steady grace.

People often think spirituality makes you detached from life. For me, it did the opposite. It made me more present. More aware. More grateful. When you've watched illness up close, when you've seen someone give their life for another without expecting anything in return, when you've experienced healing that goes beyond logic, you stop taking things lightly.

You stop complaining about small problems. You stop overreacting to situations that don't matter. You start noticing moments that do.

My journey taught me that spirituality isn't about escaping life.

It's about facing it with a stronger heart.

That doesn't mean I walk around with divine confidence every day. I still worry. I still have doubts. I still get frustrated. I'm human. But somewhere beneath all of that, there is a core that doesn't shake anymore. A part of me that knows, no matter how hard things get, I am not walking alone.

And that, to me, is the greatest miracle of all.

My spiritualism is simple:
Show up with honesty. Do the work with sincerity. Accept what comes. Let go of what you cannot control.
Amarpreet Singh Puri

Chapter 6

When the Body Speaks

I have lived through difficult phases before, but nothing prepares you for the moment your own body turns into a question you cannot answer. Illness inside the house is one thing. Illness inside your own body is something else entirely. It tests you in a way that doesn't leave room for pretending. It brings fear close to your face. And most of all, it forces you to listen: to yourself, to time, and to things you had been avoiding.

My kidney journey didn't begin suddenly. It built up quietly, the way most real problems do.

- Small signs.
- Occasional discomfort.
- A feeling that something wasn't right.

But I brushed everything aside and kept moving, the way we all do when life is busy, and responsibilities don't pause just because the body is asking for attention.

It was during a trip to Cochin that the hints became too loud to ignore. What started as mild discomfort grew into something persistent. Doctors there initially said it was likely a stone problem and sent me for more tests. But my discomfort didn't match their casual explanation. Something in me knew there was more to it.

When I returned home, I went to AIIMS. The doctors there didn't take long to detect the real issue.

I still remember the expression on the surgeon's face when he

looked at the scans, quiet, serious, the kind of look that tells you the truth before the words do.

One kidney had almost shut down. They told me directly that it had stopped functioning properly.

In that moment, fear arrived, not the loud, dramatic kind, but the slow, sinking kind that settles inside you. I wasn't thinking about the future. I was thinking about my family. About the responsibilities on my shoulders. About the people who depended on me. About the possibility that I might not be able to continue life the way I had always taken for granted.

They planned for surgery immediately. There were tests after tests. Eight different reports within days. Every number felt like a countdown.

During that phase, my days were normal on the outside.

I still worked, still met people, still responded to calls, still fulfilled commitments.

But internally, I was walking around with a constant tightening in my chest.

I started noticing every small shift in my body. Every ache felt magnified. Every quiet moment became a place where fear tried to grow.

What made it worse was that I had already seen illness up close, my mother's health crisis, the maid's cancer. I knew what a bad medical phase could do to a family. I didn't want to put mine through the same.

But life doesn't pause for your fears. It only gives you directions you didn't know you needed.

Around this time, a spiritual gathering was happening in our community, continuous Simran, Kirtan, and prayer. The environment was peaceful, the kind that affects you even before you sit down. I went there not for a miracle, but for a moment of silence within me. I needed space to breathe.

I remember standing there, surrounded by Simran's sound. It wasn't loud or dramatic. It was rhythmic. Soft. Steady. Something about that atmosphere felt different. Almost like my mind had finally stopped running. For the first time in months, I felt my anxiety loosen its grip.

And then something unexpected happened.

Within fifteen or twenty minutes, the pressure I had been carrying started to ease.

I felt lighter. I felt a kind of clarity I hadn't felt in a long time. I didn't tell anyone. I didn't make it a big moment.

But I knew something had shifted inside me.

The next morning, I went for another test, expecting the same results. But the report came back different. Clean. Numbers normal. The surgeon, who had been certain before, now looked confused. He asked for tests again. Those results came back fine, too.

Just a day before, they were preparing me for surgery.

Now, the reports showed nothing wrong.

I didn't call this a miracle loudly to anyone, but I felt the truth quietly within myself. Something had happened in that moment with Simran. Something shifted, maybe physically, maybe emotionally, maybe spiritually. But it shifted.

From that day onward, my faith changed shape. It wasn't about religion anymore. It wasn't about rituals or rules. It became something personal. Something internal. Something I carried with me rather than something I performed.

I became more mindful of my body, more respectful of my limits. I stayed a vegetarian for years. I stayed away from alcohol. I listened to myself in a way I never used to.

People think discipline is a burden, but sometimes it's what keeps you alive. Sometimes it's what brings your life back on track.

My kidney issue didn't just teach me about health. It taught me to surrender and to slow down.

Today, when I think back to that period, I don't remember the fear as much as I remember the turning point. The moment when I realised that there is a thin line between control and surrender, and sometimes, healing only happens when you stop fighting and start listening.

My body had spoken. And for the first time, I truly heard it.

Sometimes, healing only happens when you stop fighting and start listening

Amarpreet Singh Puri

Chapter 7

The Industry I Never Expected

If someone had told me in my early twenties that I would spend the next two decades of my life working with desiccants, I would have laughed. It wasn't an industry anyone dreamt of entering.

No young person ever said, "One day I want to work with moisture-control products." It wasn't glamorous, it wasn't well-known, and honestly, it didn't even sound like a real career path.

But life doesn't always open the door you expect. Sometimes it opens the one you don't notice at all until you walk through it.

After the BPO years, I was confident in my communication skills, but I didn't have a plan. I only knew one thing: I didn't want to go back to a predictable routine. I wanted to explore something that would challenge me, something that wasn't rigid or predefined. Around that time, through a buying agency, I was introduced to a company that supplied silica gel and desiccants to exporters.

I didn't know much about the product. To me, a desiccant was just a small pouch people threw away without a second thought. But exporters didn't see it that way. Their entire shipment depended on that small pouch doing its job properly. If moisture got into the cartons, everything inside could get damaged. And if that happened, the losses were massive.

So while the industry looked small from the outside, inside it was full of tension, unpredictability, and a constant need for trust.

When I joined, the company was modest. There were no huge teams, no structured departments. The office wasn't the kind with glass doors and perfect systems. It was basic, almost bare. A table, a chair, a phone, some files, and a product that most people didn't think twice about. I still remember my first day, no orientation, no welcome speech. Just direct work.

My job was simple on paper: handle exporters, understand their needs, and ensure timely supply.

In reality, it was anything but simple.

→ Exporters are under constant pressure.

→ They deal with long transit times, unpredictable weather, strict buyers, and even stricter quality control teams.

→ A single mistake can cost them a shipment.

→ So when they talk, they don't talk gently. They talk about anxiety, deadlines, frustration, and fear.

And this is where my BPO experience became my biggest strength.

I knew how to listen.

Not the "hearing words and replying fast" kind of listening.

Real listening, the kind where you understand the emotion behind the complaint.

In customer service, you learn one rule:

When someone is shouting, they're not upset with you. They're upset with their situation.

That understanding helped me survive my first few months.

Exporters would call with endless issues:

➢ Wrong pouch size

➢ Dispatch delays

- Moisture problems
- Documentation errors
- And quantity mismatches

I didn't always have the answer immediately, but what I did have was patience. And that made all the difference.

Slowly, they started trusting me. Not because we became perfect overnight, but because they knew I wouldn't disappear when something went wrong.

Trust is a strange thing. People don't give it to the smartest person. They give it to the one who stays consistent.

One of the biggest turning points came when the global buying house, the one that sourced for hundreds of stores across the US and Canada, began evaluating suppliers. They had around four hundred exporters under them.

If they trusted us, it meant we would automatically work with all those exporters.

The pressure was huge. The expectations were even bigger.

We prepared samples, answered every query, and made every minor adjustment they requested. I handled each interaction personally because I knew responsiveness builds confidence. Every email mattered. Every correction mattered. Every day mattered.

And then, one morning, the confirmation arrived. We were selected.

Overnight, the company's world changed. From handling a handful of exporters to suddenly supporting hundreds. What looked like a small product now carried the weight of global supply chains.

Work started piling up. Calls came from every direction. Exporters had different needs, different expectations, and different standards. I found myself becoming not just the sales person, but the coordinator, the planner, the documentation specialist, the relationship manager, everything at once.

We didn't have systems. So I created them.

I insisted on having a proper internet connection and a laptop, things that weren't standard in small businesses back then. I made Excel sheets to track dispatches. I organised documentation. I cleaned up the communication process. I set up a rhythm in the office so we could handle this new load without chaos.

It wasn't about being smart. It was about being willing.

Some days were overwhelming. Some days, I felt like I was holding the entire operation together by myself. But those were also the days when I understood what real work means. It's not the job someone gives you. It's the responsibility you naturally grow into.

That period taught me more than any course or training could have.

- I learned that listening solves half the problem.
- I learned that consistency wins trust.
- I learned that exporters remembered the way you handled them during the crisis more than the days when everything ran smoothly.
- I learned that small industries are actually built on big relationships.
- And most importantly, I learned that you don't need a glamorous field to build a meaningful career.

You just need one thing: commitment.

The desiccant industry wasn't something I had planned on. But it became the place where I found my footing, my confidence, and my identity.

What began as an unexpected job slowly turned into a journey that defined the next phase of my life.

And without even realizing it, I had begun walking the path that would eventually make me a partner, a leader, and someone who understood business far deeper than any textbook could teach.

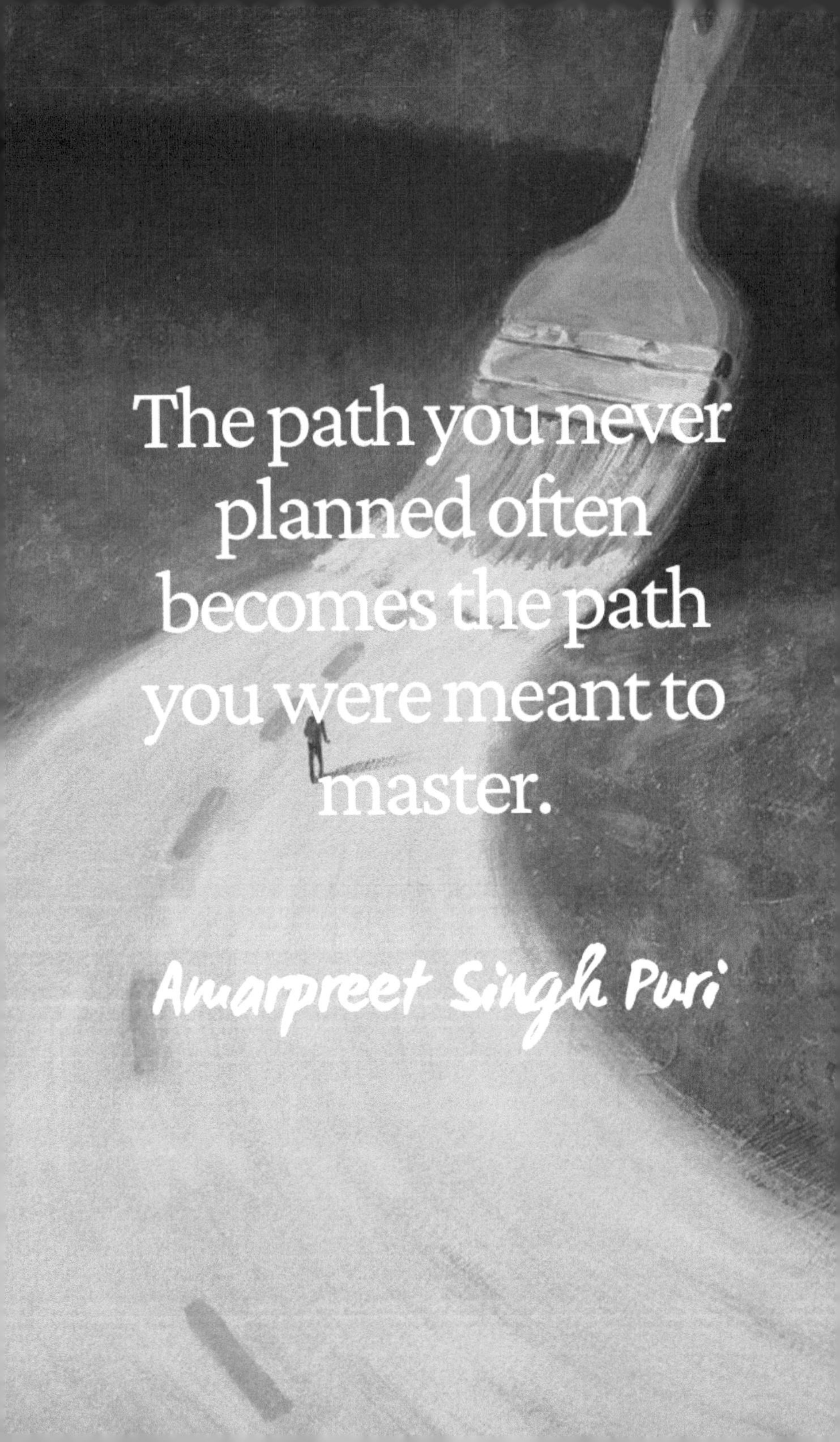
The path you never planned often becomes the path you were meant to master.
Amarpreet Singh Puri

Chapter 8

Coming Full Circle

For a long time, my work in the desiccant industry felt like the centre of my professional identity. It gave me structure, responsibility, and a sense of ownership that I had grown into slowly. I had learned how to listen, how to build trust, and how to carry accountability without needing constant validation. It was demanding work, but it was honest. And for years, that was enough.

But life has a way of reminding you that no phase is permanent.

As responsibilities at home grew and my parents aged, the idea of being closer to family began to take on a different shape. It was no longer just about being physically present. It was about being available, emotionally, mentally, and practically. I began to realise that distance does not always show up in kilometres. Sometimes it shows up in postponed decisions and responsibilities avoided.

The question was not whether I could continue doing what I was doing. The question was whether I should.

GRKC was not new to me. It had always existed in the background of my life, familiar, respected, and quietly consistent. I had seen it in conversations at home, in the way people spoke about it with trust, and in the long-standing relationships it carried. But for a long time, it remained separate from my own professional identity. Almost like something I knew deeply, yet stood outside of.

When I began stepping into GRKC more actively, I did not experience it as a return to something comfortable. I experienced it as stepping into weight. Responsibility of a different kind. The kind that does not come with experimentation or trial runs. The kind where decisions have consequences that stretch beyond the present.

The transition was not smooth.

I had spent years building my own way of working. At GRKC, those systems already existed, shaped by decades of experience, relationships, and hard-earned credibility. My first instinct was not to change anything. It was to understand why things were done the way they were.

So I slowed down.

- I watched how decisions were taken.
- I listened to how people spoke, inside and outside the organization.
- I noticed what was said openly and what was understood without words.

That period reminded me of my early days in the desiccant industry, when listening mattered more than speaking. Once again, observation became my entry point.

What surprised me most was how familiar the discomfort felt.

- The uncertainty.
- The self-doubt.
- The quiet pressure to prove that I belonged.

I realized then that growth often looks like repetition being tested again, but at a higher level. The lessons remain the same. Only the stakes change.

Years of working with exporters had taught me reliability, not as a concept, but as a daily discipline.

Years of handling complaints had taught me emotional control, especially when emotions ran high. Years of operating without shortcuts had taught me patience, even when speed seemed tempting. These were not skills you put on a résumé, but they showed up every day, in meetings, in operations, in how problems were addressed instead of avoided.

At GRKC, my thinking shifted.

- I began to care less about expansion and more about continuity.
- Less about scale and more about consistency.
- Less about visibility and more about credibility.

I understood that growth without grounding can undo years of trust. And trust, once broken, does not return easily.

There were moments of hesitation. Moments when I questioned whether I was stepping into something too layered, too complex, too demanding. Moments when I wondered if staying in a familiar professional identity would have been easier.

But those doubts were not new.

They reminded me of every turning point I had walked through before.

By then, I had learned that clarity does not arrive before effort. It arrives because of it. Waiting for certainty had never served me. Showing up had.

This phase taught me something important about legacy.

Legacy is not something you inherit and preserve.

It is something you participate in and protect.

It is built in everyday choices how you treat people, how you respond under pressure, how you handle responsibility when no one is watching.

Stepping into GRKC felt like alignment.

- With my values.
- With my responsibilities.
- With the person, life has shaped me over time.

Once again, there was no grand announcement. No dramatic moment. Just a quiet decision to take the next step, honestly.

And once again, I kept walking.

Every turning point tests old lessons at higher stakes.

Amarpreet Singh Puri

Chapter 9

ADHD, Learning the Language of My Mind

→ For most of my life, I thought I had a consistency problem.

→ Not a capability issue. Not a motivation issue. A reliability issue.

I could be sharp in meetings, thoughtful in conversations, and creative under pressure. Yet I struggled with follow-ups, timelines, and routine execution.

People trusted my thinking, but quietly stopped trusting my delivery.

I remember being told, more than once,

"You are brilliant when you show up."

What stayed with me was not the compliment.

It was the implication.

School taught me I was "underperforming."

In school, my performance never matched my understanding.

I could grasp concepts quickly in class discussions, often before others did. But homework was erratic. Projects were either overdone at the last minute or never submitted. Teachers described me as "capable but inconsistent."

Parent-teacher meetings followed a pattern.

→ "He understands everything."

→ "He just does not apply himself."

No one questioned why the application felt harder than comprehension. Neither did I. I simply assumed I was careless with potential.

Early work life made it worse

The gap widened once I entered professional environments.

In roles where expectations were vague and timelines were long, I struggled. I delayed tasks not because I forgot them, but because starting felt heavy. Emails sat unread. Follow-ups stayed unsent. I carried mental to-do lists that never fully cleared.

Ironically, in moments of crisis, I thrived.

When something broke, when a decision had to be made quickly, when pressure compressed time, I was calm, decisive, and effective. People noticed that version of me.

What they did not see was the cost.

After those bursts of performance came exhaustion. Long stretches where even simple tasks felt overwhelming. I could not explain why. So I did what many people do: I hid it.

There was a moment, much later, when the pattern became impossible to dismiss.

I had committed to something important. I cared deeply about it. I had the time. I had the ability. And yet, days passed without progress.

I was not distracted. I was stuck.

That was the first time I realised this was no longer about effort. I was trying constantly. Mentally. Emotionally. Nothing was moving.

That moment did not diagnose ADHD.

But it cracked the story I had been telling myself.

ADHD showed up quietly in my relationships, too.

I forgot things that mattered. Missed messages. Delayed replies. Not because I did not care, often because I cared too much and wanted to respond "properly."

Feedback stayed with me longer than it should have. Even well-intentioned comments replayed in my head. I learned to over-explain myself so people would not misinterpret my silences or delays.

I was always managing perception, trying to make sure my intentions were not misunderstood.

That constant self-monitoring was exhausting.

Learning about ADHD did not feel like a discovery. It felt like recognition.

For the first time, my life made sense as a whole, not as a series of isolated failures, but as one consistent pattern explained by how my brain regulates attention, initiation, and emotion.

→ What I had called laziness was executive dysfunction.

→ What I had called sensitivity was, in fact, emotional dysregulation.

→ What I had called inconsistency was a nervous system driven by engagement, not importance.

Nothing about my past changed. But the meaning of it did.

Redesigning life after understanding

The biggest shift came when I stopped asking,

"How do I force myself to be consistent?"

And started asking,

"How do I build a life that works with my brain?"

- I externalised structure.
- Reduced cognitive load.
- Stopped relying on memory for important things.
- Built systems that created momentum instead of shame.
- I learned to respect my energy rather than constantly override it.

The difference was not immediate.

But it was sustainable.

This chapter exists because many people live the way I did, functional on the outside, confused and self-critical on the inside.

→ They are not failing.

→ They are unsupported.

ADHD does not need to be romanticised or minimised. It needs to be understood, especially by adults who were never given language for their experience.

I am writing this not to rewrite my past, but to name it honestly.

Once I understood my mind, I stopped fighting it.

And that changed everything.

Behind every 'inconsistent' adult is a nervous system doing its best.

Amarpreet Singh Puri

Chapter 10

Just Walk

If there is one thing life has taught me, it is this: most answers do not arrive the way we imagine them.

I spent years believing that clarity would come first, that once things made sense, movement would follow. Experience proved the opposite. Movement came first. Understanding followed later.

I did not walk through life with a map. I walked through it with responsibility, sometimes willingly, sometimes because there was no other option. Illness entered my home. Then it entered my own body. Work demanded consistency even when certainty was missing. Faith entered my life not as belief, but as experience.

There were moments when I wanted life to slow down. Moments when I wanted guarantees. Moments when stopping felt easier than continuing.

But stopping never gave me peace. Walking did.

→ Walking taught me patience.

→ Walking taught me surrender.

→ Walking taught me that effort does not always show results immediately, but it always leaves an imprint.

Over time, I stopped asking life to explain itself to me. I stopped trying to control outcomes. I began focusing on what was in front of me, the work of the day, the responsibility of the moment, the discipline required to keep going even when motivation was absent.

That is when things began to shift.

Not suddenly.Not dramatically.But steadily.

I realised that life does not reward urgency. It responds to consistency. It does not move faster when you panic. It moves when you stay present. Many of the answers I once chased arrived quietly, long after I had stopped demanding them.

This book is not a record of achievements. It is a record of movement.

- Of continuing forward when answers were incomplete.
- Of trusting discipline over impulse.
- Of choosing faith over fear, even when faith did not come with explanations.

If you are reading this book at a time when life feels unclear, I want you to know this: uncertainty does not mean you are doing something wrong. It often means you are in the middle of becoming someone new.

- You do not need to solve everything today.
- You do not need to be fearless.
- You do not need to feel ready.

You only need to be honest with the steps you are taking.

- You may be walking through illness.
- You may be walking through responsibility.
- You may be walking through doubt, loss, or change.

Wherever you are, movement matters.

- Do not wait for perfect conditions.
- Do not wait for approval.
- Do not wait for certainty.

- Walk when the road feels uneven.
- Walk when progress feels invisible.
- Walk when faith feels quiet rather than loud.

Life does not unfold all at once.

It reveals itself step by step, often in hindsight.

And sometimes, the bravest thing you can do is not to rush ahead or turn back, but to stay with the path you are on, one honest step at a time.

That is all I have done.

That is all this book asks of you.

Just walk.....

Just Walk!
Amarpreet Singh Puri

Epilogue

There is no final moment where everything settles.

Life does not arrive at a place where all questions are answered, and nothing remains uncertain.

Even now, as I write this, there are parts of the road ahead I cannot see.

There are responsibilities still unfolding, decisions yet to be made, and lessons I have not learned fully.

And that is alright.

What has changed is not the presence of uncertainty, but my relationship with it. I no longer see unanswered questions as obstacles. I see them as part of a movement. As proof that life is still in motion.

Walking has taught me that progress is often invisible in the moment. You feel it only when you pause and look back at the distance covered, the strength built quietly, the resilience you did not know you had when the journey began.

There were times I walked out of necessity.

→ Times I walked out of duty.

→ Times I walked out of faith.

All of them mattered.

If this book ends here, it is only because a page must end somewhere. The walk does not. It continues, through ordinary days, familiar responsibilities, and moments that do not announce their importance until much later.

If you take anything from these pages, let it be this: you do not need certainty to move forward. You only need sincerity.

And when the road feels long or unclear, return to the simplest thing you can do.

Take the next step.

What People Say About Amarpreet and This Book

An Attentive Mentee, A True-Blue Singh!

Amarpreet, I am proud of you and your relentless hard work, one of my mentees who listens with intent and executes with the spirit of a true Singh.

Chardi Kala always.

~ Avijit Arya

Business Coach

A Neighbour and Friend: A Pillar of Quiet Strength

I have known Amarpreet Singh not only as a neighbour, but as a friend whose quiet strength has always stood out. Long before this book, I witnessed in him a rare steadiness, the ability to keep moving forward regardless of circumstance.

What makes Amarpreet remarkable is not loud achievement, but consistent character. He has faced life with dignity, responsibility, and faith, and this book is simply an extension of the way he lives.

Just Walk is not only his story; it is a reminder that progress is built through perseverance, honesty, and courage.

I am proud to have shared a chapter of life living next door to him, and even prouder to see his experiences now guiding others. May this book reach every person who needs the strength to take the next step.

~ Sanjay Anand

Hammer Publishers

A Deeply Relatable and Inspiring Book

This book is deeply inspiring.

There were many moments when it felt as though Amarpreet was telling my own life story. It moved me profoundly.

I wish him every success. This book will surely go far in inspiring countless readers.

Thank you for sharing your journey with such honesty, and for reminding us that sometimes, all we truly need to do... is keep walking.

~ Nitin Gupta

Export Marketing Coach

A Mannat Child Serving With Humility

History shows us that walking for a cause has shaped humanity's greatest transformations. Amarpreet continues that tradition, whether navigating ADHD, living with quiet strength, or serving others with humility.

I first saw the spark in his eyes when he was my Grade 3 student, a spark that still illuminates his path of service today. He walked beside me while donating blood, and later walked me through life when I was in the depths of sorrow.

So... just walk.

May God always walk with this Mannat child.

~ Manmeen Kaur Oberoi

Educator (Amarpreet's SST Teacher)

This book feels like a hand held in silence when words fall short.

It carries pain, faith, and endurance without ever asking for sympathy.

The writing does not rush healing; it stays with you until you are ready to move again.

You don't finish this book feeling transformed.

You finish it feeling less alone.

~ Prateek Garg

Elatio Homes

An Honest & Empowering Reflection

Life rarely unfolds in straight lines. It bends, pauses, and sometimes breaks us open in ways we never imagined. In Just Walk, Amarpreet Singh Puri invites us into those bends and pauses, not as a teacher with formulas, but as a fellow traveler who has stumbled, endured, and kept moving.

I have known Amarpreet personally for many years and have witnessed him face some of life's most difficult challenges with remarkable courage and resilience. His first-person account of how he navigated those trials and emerged stronger is not only inspiring but also deeply moving. This book is a testament to his strength and perseverance.

Just Walk is not about extraordinary achievements or dramatic victories. It is about the quiet courage of persistence, the strength found in responsibility, and the grace of continuing when clarity is absent. Amarpreet's journey through illness, family obligations, professional challenges, and spiritual searching reminds us that progress is not always loud. Sometimes, it is simply the decision to take one more step.

What makes Just Walk deeply resonant is its honesty. Amarpreet does not hide the weight of expectations, the storms of self-doubt, or the fractures of health and circumstance. Instead, he shows us how endurance, faith, and love can transform those struggles into lessons. His reflections are not prescriptions; they are invitations to slow down, to reflect, and to trust that walking itself can be enough.

For anyone standing at a crossroads, waiting for certainty, this book offers a gentle reminder: clarity often comes after movement, not before. Amarpreet's words carry the lived truth that transitions require patience, and that even in uncertainty, we are not failing; we are walking.

May these pages encourage you to keep moving forward, one step at a time. Just Keep Walking.

~ Amarjit Singh Lamba

Major General(Retd.) (Amarpreet's Father-in-Law)

A Self-Made & Responsible Individual Rooted In Values

I was Amarpreet's mathematics teacher and class teacher during his school years. He was part of the very first senior secondary batch of our school and later became its first Head Boy. Even as a student, he was sincere, disciplined, and extremely responsible - someone who could always be relied upon, both inside and outside the classroom.

He had a caring and respectful nature and was always mindful of the people around him. He carried strong values, followed discipline naturally, and showed maturity beyond his age. His proficiency as a tabla player and his religious inclination reflected his balanced upbringing and grounded personality.

Reading about his life journey today does not surprise me. The values and the inner strength I saw in him as a student are the same ones that have helped him face life's challenges with dignity and humility. Despite many ups and downs, he has remained rooted, committed to his family and true to himself.

As a teacher, I feel proud to have taught him and to see how he has grown into a self-made and responsible individual. This book is a true reflection of the person he has always been.

I wish him all the very best in life and for this book.

~ Meeta Sodhi

Educator (Amarpreet's Class Teacher & Mathematics Teacher)

A Great Job!

Dear Amar,

Great Job! Thrilled to witness your journey and your transformation.

~ Akshar Yadav

Marketing Guru, Creator of The Get Overbooked Marketing Framework

I am truly proud of you and your family for the perseverance, courage, and commitment that have shaped this remarkable journey of learning and growth.I am genuinely moved. Your openness to learning and your humility in the face of life's challenges will inspire countless readers who witness your process of evolution through these pages.

Dr. Siddhart Chellani, Sambhav Clinic